A Routine Interrupted

How Fasting Changed Everything

———————————————

Leticia C. Odametey

Disclaimer

The content of this book is not intended to be a guide to medical treatment for any diagnosis. These are my individual experiences, led by God, in treating my son with autism.

Please consult with a health professional to determine if any supplements, diets, and/or medical approaches are necessary for your child.

Unless otherwise noted, all Scripture quotations are from the New King James Version of the Bible.

DeDiCaTIoN

I give thanks to God first and foremost. Without Him, nothing would be possible. He set the tone for the course of my life by giving me my Jewel, Jordan.

My family, I can't thank God enough for surrounding me with a bunch of ME's. To have you all act as silly as I do gets me through a lot of tough times. Damecia, my twin, you give me life. Thank you for being you and always being genuine. Sierra, you keep me on my toes, but you are a fantastic soul. You encourage me at times, and you don't even know it. Thank you. Michayla, I am honored to be your second mom. You are there to talk to when I need it most and a blessing to my life. Kaiyah, I don't have enough space to say what I want to say about our relationship. You were the little one who came along after Jordan. It seemed like he spoke to me through you. Those moments I wished I could hear him say, I love you; you said it almost instantaneously. You have been such a tremendous help with your big brother. I am amazed you are my baby girl. Don, what can I say about my other half that I haven't already said. Our marriage has been a character builder for sure, but I wouldn't want to have anybody else by my side. Thank you for being you.

Jordan, one day you will be able to read this and understand everything I did was because of you. You are my reason for being. You may make me "uppaset" when you act out, but overall, you make me happy. Thank you for showing me love in a SPECIAL way.

I LOVE YOU ALL

a roUTiNe iNTErUpPTeD

How **Fasting** cHANGED <u>everything</u>

TaBLe oF COntEnTs

Introduction

Chapter 1: The birth of a routine interrupted

Chapter 2: How treatment led to finding God

Chapter 3: Before the fast

Chapter 4: What I learned in the beginning stages

Chapter 5: Distractions

Chapter 6: When fasting was over

Chapter 7: Finding God's diet through fasting

Chapter 8: Getting started

Chapter 9: Getting stuck

Chapter 10: Giving up more

Chapter 11: The unexpected

Chapter 12: Finding the root of it all

Chapter 13: Something new

Chapter 14: From doubting to clarity

Chapter 15: Learning patience

Chapter 16: Improvement

Chapter 17: Time to be quiet

Chapter 18: Other POV's

Chapter 19: Donald

Chapter 20: Tionn'es Q&A

Chapter 21: Sierra

Chapter 22: Kaiyah's Q&A

Chapter 23: Loretta

In closing

Last thoughts

InTRoduCtion

If we think about it, life is one big routine. We are born, created with a purpose, of course. We live, and we live again. By live again, I mean we go on to be with the Heavenly Father after our life on earth ends.

In between being born and transitioning into eternal life, we have what I like to call a routine. We go to school, make friends, get into trouble, go to school more, have a career, pay bills, find your mate, get married, have kids, retire, have grandkids and wait for the good Lord to call us home. That can be some people's view of what happens in a typical life. Then some lives are not so "normal." The lives of those who somewhere in between getting married and retiring have kids that are a bit different. They may have a learning disability or Cerebral Palsy. Some with Down Syndrome, and others may have Spina Bifida. I happen to be one of those parents who is raising a child with autism.

Technically, autism is defined as a mental disorder present from early childhood, characterized by difficulty communicating and forming relationships with other people and using language and abstract concepts. However, in treating my son, I have learned that while most think autism is neurological, it is an autoimmune disorder. Either way, I define autism as my lifesaver. If it weren't for my son being differently abled, I might not have built the relationship I have with God and found the calling He placed on my life.

Most times, we look at life's interruptions as a huge hassle. When your car breaks down, the inconvenience and the extra money you must pay to get it fixed that you weren't planning on spending is a hassle that comes to mind. But this could be God's way of doing numerous things to protect you from dangers unseen. One could be the fact that you could have ended up being in a fatal accident. It also could be the sign of a more severe problem that your car is facing, and this warning could have saved you from breaking down somewhere far from home or something even worse. Lastly, it could be God's way of getting your attention because you are distracted. God tries to get our attention when we are probably not on the right road and need to get there before it's too late.

Now I've learned to embrace my interruptions. Fasting is an interruption in our routine that we place before ourselves to get closer to God. Last year I completed a 40-day fast that changed the dynamic of everything I was doing to treat Jordan. This book will take you through the journey. Originally the book was supposed to share with you the many ways my routines had been interrupted by life. But just as the title explains, something happened that made me change it for the third time. First, let me share with you the interruption that got me here.

Chapter 1

"The birth of a routine interrupted"

On a chilly September morning, I was doing my morning routine. I had dropped my second grader off at school already, and now it was time to continue with Jordan and getting him ready for the bus.

Usually, after homework and getting dressed, he comes down to get a little time on his tablet. In the last few days, he had been playing Temple Run instead of listening to the Chipmunks. His dad just started a new job, which caused him to wake up a little earlier than he used to. So, while Jordan usually brings his tablet in the kitchen with him to take his supplements and set it off to the side right before breakfast, dad didn't allow him to take it out of the living room at all. Now I understand why, but I let him because we *are* talking about Jordan.

Jordan doesn't have a problem needing to stick to routines as much as he used to, but the issue is still there. I guess it all depends on what is being interrupted. There are plenty of days where he hasn't followed his routine. A while ago, he stopped going straight upstairs after school to change his clothes and went into the den for a few minutes. I don't know what caused him to do things differently for those days, but it's what suited him at the time. Something else that doesn't bother him is the car he rides in. My SUV had been having issues at one time. It went from the wheel bearings to the brakes to a tune-up, and lastly, the rotors were replaced. But he can get into my mother's car and even his uncles with no problems. Some kids just won't change up as easily as he does. I'm so thankful for his easy-going spirit at times. This morning wasn't one of those times, though.

While Jordan didn't give me too much of a challenging time that morning, he did show his agitation. He whined when I gave him his supplements and didn't do his usual tasks as smoothly as he usually does. For example, when I noticed his undershirt was on backward and inside out, he took his outer shirt off right away. However, putting everything back on was an unnecessary, drawn-out process. He took a long time tucking the undershirt back in, paused a few times, putting on his uniform shirt, and sat down on the floor before doing it.

Afterward, it was time to eat, and he didn't want to pick up his plate to bring it to the dining room, even though he's the only one that can do it, according to him. He pulled out the syrup for his French toast sticks, although he had done it earlier, and it had been poured on his food already. When he finally sat down to eat, he was okay if dad was in the house. As soon as his father stepped out and I stepped away to finish making his lunch, the disturbed Jordan showed up again. He tried to rip some coupons I had sitting on the table. When I stopped him from doing that, he knocked over my water bottle. Since I wanted him to hurry up and eat because the bus can come early, I sat with him to keep him on track. He continued to whine until he was almost done. That's when I got up to finish what I was doing. After I moved, he stood up and pointed to the living room, saying, "Loud House," a cartoon he watches on the Nick app. I told him no Loud House, and he sat down and finished his food so he could go get his tablet until the bus came. He whined a little bit more, but that was the extent of it. All things considered, it could have been worse.

While I was sitting with Jordan when he was eating, I thought about how my morning was interrupted because of the discipline dad gave to him that threw him off just a bit. It began to weigh on me a little because while dad plays a significant role in Jordan's life, it's hard for me when he corrects Jordan, and I'm left to deal with the consequences. This is not the first time I have felt like that.

About a year or so ago, when I tried to follow dad's lead when it came to Jordan, it didn't go over so well. I tried to get Jordan out of this bathroom routine he had. This time it was right before bed, and dad also heard and saw what was going on and intervened. When Jordan didn't get to follow his routine, he sat in bed that entire night crying and pulling the covers on and off him and hitting himself. I tried not to give in and laid with him until he went to sleep, but he just couldn't. I can't remember how late it was, but I finally let him have his way. He probably didn't get to sleep until about 5 in the morning. And then had to wake up close to 7 o'clock for school. That's when it first came to me that dad doesn't have to deal with the issues that follow interruptions as I do. I decided that I wasn't going to go through that again. Jordan can follow any routine he wants as long as it's not life-threatening.

That morning's response to the routine change wasn't as bad as the ones prior, but it made me realize that when Jordan strays from routines because of his father's commands, he does it willingly because of his fear of him. Don, his father, is the only person he will comply with like that. Not teachers, not his grandmother or uncle, and not me. That speaks volumes to me. That's the kind of fear we as children of God have of our Father. We are so concerned about the punishment for our wrong behaviors that we get in line only from the mere thought of Him. However, because He gives free will, sometimes we choose whether we follow His precepts or not. Once we choose, we must deal with the consequences of our actions. Jordan doesn't want to deal with the results of not obeying his father's word, so he follows his commands and even thinks twice about doing wrong when dad is around. But, when he's not in his presence, he is just like a person who behaves appropriately while in the church because it's God's house. And as soon as they step out, they proceed to act as if God isn't there. But God is always there, and we should behave as such, not only when we think He is looking.

When my husband didn't allow my son to go through his usual ritual, the outcome from it made all these thoughts come to mind and led me to want to blog. This is how "A Routine Interrupted" came to be.

Chapter II

"How treatment led to finding God"

I was on the path of helping Jordan get to the point where Jordan's diagnosis of autism was no longer needed.

Jordan's treatment consisted of a gluten-free diet, supplements that increased about every three months, and chelation. The diet allowed Jordan to sleep through the night, which was great. Nor more waking up at 3 or 4 in the morning to play. Supplements were a bit of a struggle. Before I removed them, he was taking a total of 23 supplements, and most of them twice a day. Not only did I feel it was too expensive, I thought it was too much for him. Also, every time I introduced a new one to him, it would do the job it is supposed to for a brief time, then he would go back to how he was before.

I saw the most significant gains during the chelation process. Chelation removes heavy metals from the body in numerous places due to the body not properly disposing of them. Jordan's levels of lead would fluctuate. They would go down, but they would skyrocket even though I did not do anything different in the following three months. However, he would continue to lose some of his autistic characteristics. He started to give great eye contact; straying from routine did not frustrate him as much and the list of foods he would eat increased tremendously. He went from eating just pizza, chicken nuggets, hot gods, and waffles to hamburgers, not dos on a bun, spaghetti, black beans, spinach, and a host of other vegetables.

Jordan's 5th grade school year was when it all started to come to a head. He began to misbehave in embarrassing ways. There were instances of him throwing pencils and spitting at teachers. I tried my best to develop resolutions such as increasing calming supplements and reducing sugary foods to give him a more balanced blood sugar level. When those techniques didn't work, I added fiber to aid. It did the trick, but adding too much fiber caused other problems. Once I concluded that Jordan consuming fiber was a significant issue, not only because giving him too much made him dehydrated, but it also hindered him from getting the proper nutrients he needed from food.

Discontinuing the fiber cause the negatives behaviors to return. Since I couldn't give the fiber in a supplement form, I decided to provide more fiber in the foods eaten. It started with the sautéed spinach and black beans. I found the problem with giving fiber in foods, you must find the proper ratio for it to do its job, and I just couldn't find the right one. Giving these foods wasn't a total loss, but you never knew which Jordan you were getting from day to day as far as his behaviors went. I honestly was at a loss as to what to do to get them under control.

Shortly after, I started attending church regularly, but without my family. I was going because I felt lost, but I wanted us to worship together after some time. However, having a child with special needs made it difficult.

The church I attend has over 119 ministries, but I did not see one to help families go to services that had children with special needs. When I approached the ministry support office about perhaps starting one, I was advised there was already one in place.

I joined the Special Needs ministry and became so involved that my family didn't worship with me. On the other hand, my relationship with Christ changed by putting God first, reading the Word, praying in faith, fellowshipping with others, and witnessing to the world (the principles taught in book 1, The Disciples Cross[1] in the discipleship class I took in 2015.) With that vertical being in order, Jordan's results decreased regularly. So, instead of going up, down, and up again, the lead levels consistently declined. The key the entire time was God. Ever since, I haven't had any doubt that God can't make the impossible

---

[1] Willis Jr., Avery T. "Masterlife: The Disciples Cross (Book 1)". Adult Ministry Publishing. Nashville, TN, (1996)

possible.

However, that doesn't mean that I haven't come across any snags. Along the way was when Jordan developed the behavioral problems I discussed earlier. I dealt with notes home from school, problems on the bus, and even misbehavior when I had to leave him alone with his older siblings. It got to the point where I wouldn't go anywhere, or if I did, I would take him along with me just so I didn't have to worry about what he would do at home. This issue went on for many years. But being with God allowed for these things to become more comfortable to handle over time and led me to the next steps I needed to do in my walk.

Chapter Three

"Before the fast"

What I was doing to recover or heal Jordan was not easy because it can be a very controversial issue. But the way I look at life is not one of a worldly view, but one of a spiritual perspective.

The book of Mark, written by an unknown author, chapter 9, tells a story about a healed boy. He was mute and, from the description, also had seizures. Those two characteristics are seen in some children with autism. Jesus healed him by calling for a *"deaf and dumb spirit to come out of him and enter him no more." (Mark 9:26)*. The disciples tried to cast it out to no avail and asked Jesus how he could do so. *Mark 9:29 "So he said to them this kind can come out by nothing but prayer and fasting."* Ever since I came across that verse in the Bible, I have chosen to believe my God can do the unthinkable and heal my son. It doesn't matter what the world says.

However, I needed to take the next steps and implement fasting. In September 2016, I decided to participate in a worldwide 40-Day Surrender fast held by FBCG and Dr. Celeste Owens, author of the 40-Day Surrender Fast.

There were guidelines we had to follow before fasting. One is to seek God for guidance[1]. I had to ask Him what He wanted me to give up instead of fasting from what I wanted to. When you think of fasting, you think of turning down your plate, but it doesn't have to be and shouldn't always be food.

---

[1] Owens Ph.D., Celeste "The 40-Day Surrender Fast". Good Success Publishing. Oxon Hill, MD (2011), 4

When we decide to fast, we need to consult with God so He can tell us what is consuming us and what we need to remove for a time. I had an idea of what I wanted to give up, but I wasn't sure if it was of God or what I wanted. Then he confirmed it for me on two separate occasions. One was a brief clip of our Bible study that introduced the fast, and the other from the facilitator over the class I was assisting in. Both said, turn the TV off. And that is what I had in mind.

I felt right about surrendering this because anyone that knows me knows that I am a sports fanatic. I watched basketball and wrestling in my elementary and teenage years and football with a bit of baseball in high school and after. I looked forward to the next season as soon as the super bowl was over. I was indeed giving up something that meant a lot to me.

At first, I thought it would be a huge struggle, but when you do what God has asked of you, He gives you the provisions to get through it all. And even though I knew I would be able to get through it, I was a little down about giving it up. Instead of watching TV every Sunday afternoon, I would need to find something constructive to do during this time.

When I decided to fast for 40 days, I felt I needed work handling the finances differently. I made improvements, but there was always room to get better. I felt now was a good of a time as any to figure out how to become and stay a good steward over what He has given us. I was looking forward to reading and enlightening myself on those days when I would not be in front of the TV. I knew it was something my husband would be grateful for because, as overseer of the finances, I can lose track of what goes out, and a lot of times, our account would overdraw. I know it was very frustrating to him, although he handled it with much patience.

Since I decided to give up TV and focus on finances during the downtime, I was excited to get things going. All I needed to do now was to find the proper materials to read. I couldn't wait to see how being obedient in this area of my life would bless my family and me.

Chapter 4

"What I learned in the beginning stages"

Since I would be without TV and social media for an extended time, I now needed to find something to do during this time of being idle. I needed to get that book I said I would read. After deciding finances is what I wanted to improve on after my fast was over, you would think that is what I would get a spiritual book on. However, when it was time to make my purchase, I went for a book relating to autism.

Getting to the root of Jordan's behavioral problem has been a struggle of mine for a while, and I think God felt this was the time to find the source, not focus on finances. His behaviors were still the same and had been for some time, so trying to better our funds would not solve that problem. Since God always knows best, He took control, and I ended up purchasing what would help me find what I needed to get Jordan to behave better. The book, entitled "The Un-Prescription for Autism"[1], by Janet Lintala, was a very eye-opening one and was the beginning of an exciting journey about food and healing.

I had come across many presentations about how food is medicine. Long before we had man-made remedies, we had to rely on healing by way of nature. There are lots of foods shaped like the organs of the body they help. Cut carrots look like the eye and help promote eye health and protect vision. Celery is shaped like bones, and both are 23% sodium. When you don't have enough sodium in your body, it pulls it from

---

[1] Lintala, Janet with Murphy, Martha W. "The Un-Prescription for Autism" AMACOM, New York, NY (2016)

your bones. There are numerous veggies that I could list, but I think you get the idea.

This author shared a lot about what she did to help her son and lessen the symptoms of autism. One of the things she talked about was the Feingold diet (FD). It removes artificial ingredients and foods that have a natural substance called salicylates[2]. These elements have been found to cause some to have ADHD and behavioral issues. I concluded that it was one of the reasons why Jordan had started acting the way he did. His diet was steadily growing, and he was consuming more of the foods that had these ingredients in them.

It was hard trying to start Jordan on this diet because information about it is not readily available to you over the internet. To perfect it, you must purchase a membership that gives you a list of all the parent-requested foods approved to eat. It is not exclusive to being gluten or casein-free, but it will advise you if it contains it. It also has many foods on the list that can give you an issue, such as annatto, a natural coloring that some may react to negatively.

I put Jordan on this FD diet as soon as I could, but without the membership. For an extended period, Jordan only ate oatmeal with water for breakfast and baked chicken and cabbage for lunch and dinner. Behaviorally, he was at his best. Even his handwriting improved. But he wasn't getting the proper nutrients he needed due to eating the same foods for lunch and dinner. His weight stalled, and he started to have muscle spasms due to poor nutrition. I finally broke down and bought the membership, which in my opinion, was worth it, but not for the reason you might expect

Many of the approved foods listed when I gave to him caused those negative behaviors to return. I knew the diet worked because when he was on my version of the diet, which consisted of a handful of foods, he was just fine. When adding certain approved foods, the regression he had made me look more into why he was having a problem with some of

---

[2] Lintala, Janet with Murphy, Martha W. "The Un-Prescription for Autism" (Online Action Plan). AMACOM, New York, NY (2016), 41

them.

It could have been some of the natural ingredients in the foods he reacted to or the fact that I learned he was getting snacks that may have been outside both the Feingold and gluten-free diet restrictions. I found out he was getting unapproved foods one day after he got off the bus. When he spoke to me, he was eating something, and it smelled sweet. It could have been the reason for the setback, but I still felt something else played a part. After more research, I finally came across an article that gave me the real reason for it all.

If it had not been for the diet, I don't know when or if I would have found it out. Jordan was becoming sensitive to many of the foods he was eating due to him having a leaky gut. I knew it was an issue but never took the time to determine how it affected the body and related to the problems we were faced with. Jordan's body was fighting every food that was getting through to it from the gaps in the gut lining. It was time to start working on sealing his gut.

If it had not been for giving up TV and social media due to the fast, I wouldn't have had to fill my time with reading and would not have come across the book's information that leads me to this point.

Chapter 5

"Distractions"

Every Christian knows that it won't be long before you encounter strife when you start focusing on God to improve your life.

If I may be honest, this was indeed my first fast. Yes, I had fasted from food for a weekend a few times when Jordan was going through chelation because I thought it would help his results be more consistent with the decreases in his levels. But doing that was no different when I would be down and out because of my melancholic temperament. I would go for days without eating. Not purposely, but because I didn't have the energy or the want to do so.

Therefore, I consider the 40-Day Surrender fast to be my very first fast. And with it came the attacks and distractions of the enemy. Every time I felt I had him defeated, he would come back with a counter that made me want to give up again. But I never did. I always looked forward to the outcome of passing the test and kept fighting.

While I was fasting, I kept up a journal that documented my inspiration throughout it and what I was learning, and how some of the prayers I had were answered. One of them the very next day. It came on day 10 of the fast. I had been distracted that night by television. I didn't give in to watch, but in my opinion, it was worse. Let me explain to you how it all went down starting before the fast.

Jordan came to really enjoy the newest version of the cartoon, The Chipmunks, and would watch their show on the den TV every day. One time he deleted shows we recorded from the DVR for no reason. My husband and I talked with him, explaining that he is supposed to watch his saved shows and not mess with anything else. For the most part, he didn't do it again, maybe on one other occasion.

A short time into the fast, the DVR had about a week's worth of shows that my husband and I enjoyed watching together saved. Jordan decided while watching TV to delete some of the shows I planned on watching when the fast was over. My husband talked to Jordan about it, and he ended up coming upstairs with me for a few minutes before returning to the den. When he went back into the DVR this time, he deleted them entirely. My husband came upstairs and informed me of what happened, and my first thought was to search the internet to see if there were ways to restore shows after being deleted out of the DVR trash.

After some time, I realized this was something I shouldn't focus on. We shouldn't focus on what we are fasting from while fasting from it and thinking about getting back to it after the fast is over. Otherwise, we may miss what we are supposed to be learning right at that time. Matthew 6:34 *"Therefore, do not worry about tomorrow, for tomorrow will worry about its own things. Sufficient for the day is its own trouble."* I gave up trying to restore the shows and went back to my priority, fasting.

During my devotional with the journal, some of the reflections that we had to do were about being productive or busy, being busy for the sake of being busy, rest and renewal, and what activities are the Holy Spirit urging us to eliminate. But the lesson for day 10, Renewal is Necessary[1], was so eye-opening I had no choice but to see God's hand in this.

My daily prayer was to stay strong during the fast and not return to the shows that were unpleasing to Him. God showed me one better and had my son remove them. It had to be Him because when Jordan deleted shows, he never went into the recent deletes and deleted it from there too. He also never went back and removed anything after we told him not to.

---

[1] Owens Ph.D., Dr. Celeste "The 40-Day Surrender Fast". Good Success Publishing. Oxon Hill, MD (2011), 59

For this to occur, it had to be something that the Lord commanded Jordan to do on behalf of what I prayed. It's funny how sometimes we ask God for something, and when He answers, we fight it.

I didn't realize what had occurred until the next day when continuing in the lesson. When I looked back to my prayer, I realized this was what I asked. The deleted shows were shows that I would not go back to once the fast was over. No more watching Grey's Anatomy, How to Get Away with Murder, Steve Wilkos, and whatever else I liked to watch. Those shows were just distractions anyway. Now during the day, I can do something productive like writing or spending time with the Master.

We must consider if what we are doing, day to day, moment to moment, benefiting the kingdom of God. Of course, we can have our time to enjoy life, times where spirituality isn't the only focus, but we still should make sure that it isn't immoral or conflicts with what His Word teaches. If we enjoy things that are unpleasing to Him, we become accepting of those things, and that's just as bad as participating in the sin.

But please don't mistake what I am saying as me portraying I am perfect. *"For all have sinned and fall short of the glory of God,"* Romans 3:23. I sin, just like everyone else in the world. I know I do things that aren't pleasing to Him. But I learned something invaluable in that lesson that makes me think long and hard about the choices I make, shows I watch, things I say, and ways I act. Thankfully, He is a God of second chances. Deciding not to return to those shows allowed me to concentrate on Jordan's behaviors and diet now. Also, I would be less distracted and not worry about who will do what to who on a show.

Today I no longer look at distractions as a hassle but instead look for the lesson within them.

Chapter 6

"When fasting was over."

Sometime after the fast was over, I decided to limit the time I spent on social media. Because of the growth that was happening in me, wanting to spend time peeking into others' lives became less appealing. With the decreased amount of time I spent on my phone looking at unnecessary things, I had more time for the biggest concern in my life was.

Jordan had been on the FD for several months but would only do well with a handful of foods. The diet was yielding success with his behaviors, but there was still some regression. I knew the behavioral problem could be prevalent because we still needed to work on healing his gut. Therefore, I needed to find what could restore a permeated gut.

After some more research, I found the GAPS diet. If you know about the GAPS diet, you know how overwhelming just thinking about starting it is. Luckily, I didn't have to take away any food he truly enjoyed, as I had already discontinued them because of the previous diet. It was almost a precursor because while he was on the FD, I found feeding him sauerkraut and yogurt supported the beneficial bacteria within the body. That is also one of the requirements of the GAPS diet. It was a smooth transition from one to the other.

Oddly enough, I had come across the GAPS diet plenty of times before deciding it was the diet to start him on. One day in November of 2016, I gathered more information, should it be the route I was directed to go in. Jordan was still on the FD, but I wanted to weigh our options for the best for him. However, when I tried to print some paperwork that explains the various stages of the GAPS diet, my laptop and printer would not connect. After trying to get it set up for what seemed like hours, I spoke to the Lord and told Him I would not be concerned with the diet right now, but I needed the printer to print something aside from it. Shortly afterward, everything connected, and I got what I needed.

To me, it was a sign that this was something He didn't want me to be concerned with. To be honest, I was a little skeptical about if I could handle the GAPS diet. This diet has six stages to the introduction of it alone. Not only did that worry me, but also what he needed to eat during each phase. I didn't think it was something that I was ready to do. I guess God felt the same way.

It wasn't until March of the following year that I was confident Jordan should be on this diet and felt I could do everything I needed to do. Where I was once concerned about sending in the soup to school for lunch, I no longer had any reservations about it.

After I concluded this was the proper diet for this time, I purchased the "Gut and Phycology Syndrome"[1] book, by Natasha Campbell-McBride, to mentally prepare for what I was about to start. Page after page, I gathered so much information that connected the dots as to why nothing I did, even supplements, worked long term. I grew more confident that this was the right way to go.

I had to sort through many options to find the right places to buy what I needed for meal preparation for the first few diet stages. Mainly where to get the beef bones that should come from a local farm. I checked out the farmer's market closest to me and online, where I found a Pennsylvania farm that delivers. But the best option was a farm that was not even 15 minutes up the road from me. They were who I decided I would purchase from and have been doing so ever since. I was now ready to start the process of repairing his gut. After the fast was over, I learned how beneficial it is in your walk with Christ.

Fasting is a way of clearing your mind of things, good or evil, which allows you to hear from God. When we clutter our minds with

---

[1] Campbell-McBride, Natasha, "Gut and Psychology Syndrome" Medinform Publishing. Cambridge, UK (2010)

irrelevant things, it doesn't make it easy for new ones to come in. When we give up something, it cleanses you in away. When we give up something, it purifies us in a sense. "Toxins" are removed, and nutritional elements replace them to give us what we need to move forth and do His will.

To hear from Him is crucial, and we will not hear when we have too many things going on. We won't know the will He has for our lives. If we don't know the He has for us, we can't be used to further His kingdom. So, we sacrifice what we want and let go of some unnecessary things to allow Him to do what He does.

I haven't been the same since fasting. My passion for God has continued to grow, and my want for Him has increased because I realized that His way is the way. I want Him to have control over my life so He can get the glory. Otherwise, I will think I did this on my own, and we all know who the credit really belongs to.

Chapter vii

"Finding God's diet through fasting"

Before the fast, and learning the GAPS diet was the proper diet, I had thought about starting Jordan on the Ketogenic diet.

I first heard about the Ketogenic diet at a ministry meeting. One of our members came to me for understanding due to her child being put on that diet. However, someone misunderstood Ketogenic for chelation, which Jordan was going through at the time, and sent her to me. I had no idea about it then but have since learned what it entails.

The Ketogenic diet is a low-carb diet that turns fat into energy. This diet is designed to raise the ketones in the body to optimal levels to help with mental and physical performance. Putting your body in a ketosis state will allow a steady flow of ketones to the brain to improve focus and concentration. I seriously considered this diet instead of the GAPS diet because of that reason alone. I wanted Jordan's brain to function as it should and believed this was the best way to do it. But I have since learned that I can't put Jordan on the diet I want him on, but the one God wants him on.

In a Bible study from March, I learned that foods are a test from God[1]. The book of Danie is an example of that. Daniel and three other sons of Judah, along with other children of Israel and some king's descendants, were brought to King Nebuchadnezzar's palace. They were young men, without blemish, that were quick to understand, knowledgeable, and had the ability to serve. The king appointed them a

---

[1] Owens, Dr. Celeste "Restoration of Health through Surrender" Pt. 2. First Baptist Church of Glenarden Bible Study, Upper Marlboro, MD (March 31, 2015)

daily provision of his delicacies. However, Daniel vowed to not defile himself with the king's food or wine that he drank. Because of that, God brought him into good favor. The steward set over Daniel, Hananiah, Mishael, and Azariah, allowed them to eat vegetables and drink water for ten days while the other young men ate the king's delicacies. At the end of the ten days, their appearance was better and fatter than those who did not eat the vegetables and drank water, and God gave them knowledge and skill in all literature and wisdom, and Daniel had an understanding in all visions and dreams.

Adam and Eve were also punished in the Garden of Eden due to eating the forbidden fruit. God has a specific diet for each of us, and we should consult Him to find out what it is.

The reason why we should do that is that our minds can make our bodies sick. We eat many foods we want that aren't good for us and harmful to our health. Another reason why we need to ask God 80% of diseases have a spiritual root and 75-90% of illnesses are due to our thought life because what we eat is essential to God, and most people aren't eating healthy. I also learned this from the same bible study.

Before there were man-made remedies to illnesses, we ate to make ourselves well. That is because God created it that way. Just because we now have "quick fixes" or other methods of dealing with sickness doesn't mean God's course has been exhausted or should not be used. On the contrary, we should be eating in a way the keeps us from being sick in the first place, but since we don't, at least see him for the God he is and allow him to speak to you regarding your ailments, obey His word and give Him the glory when you are healed.

When I first started this journey, I had to put Jordan on a gluten-free diet. Although his tests didn't show he had an issue with gluten or casein, the doctor recommended it, so I did. The first blessing that came from that was Jordan sleeping through the night. I was amazed but still didn't realize the importance of what we put in our bodies. He continued the gluten-free diet until I found the Feingold diet that came to me during the fast.

Being on this diet improved his behaviors and his handwriting slightly. However, the only foods he could eat weren't enough to nourish his body correctly. I had to find the perfect diet for him, the one God says is for him.

After learning that the reason he could still be having behavior problems was his body attacking the food that was getting into places within him they weren't supposed to and causing backlash, I conceded GAPS was the way to go. I genuinely believe this is the diet God wants for Jordan.

Chapter Eight

"Getting started"

On April 8, 2017, I officially started Jordan on the GAPS diet after all signs pointing to it being the one.

That morning I went to the farm for bones, the organic market for vegetables then made the broth and soup. It was weird having to give Jordan soup for breakfast. But if this was going to be the way, I had to be all in. I wasn't sure how he would like it, but he warmed up to it quickly. He wasn't fond of the broth at first, but just as all the supplements he's had to take over the years, he got used to it.

After a few days in, I realized I didn't have enough beef soup for the rest of the week, so I bought a whole chicken and made chicken soup until the following Saturday when I can purchase more bones. The next week I added a fish soup made from the red snapper. He loved that the most until I made lamb soup. It was all over from there, and that was what he wanted the most.

Almost a week later, I started him on the homemade sauerkraut. He was also taking CD Biotic, one of the supplements he took before the diet. However, it gave him adverse effects, so I reduced the amount and increased it every few days. I introduced him to the fermented cod liver oil for omega 3 fatty acids and yogurt for more probiotics.

After 3 weeks on this diet, there was a considerable difference in his behaviors at school. However, they were short-lived as well. To this day, I'm still not sure what made him act out at times. He still could have been getting food outside the house, like in times prior and at home. Being as though he is the only one on a special diet in the household when food is left out that I make for others in the family, he will sneak and eat it. My husband caught him one evening, getting macaroni and cheese out of the pot on the stove.

It was evident that a more watchful eye had to be kept on him. Doing this was quite tricky because I have other things to tend to, and when I am settled for the evening, I don't think to follow Jordan's every move when he is not around me or gets up to leave the room. I now had to be conscientious of where he was within the house. That was going to take some getting used to.

Also, during the first few weeks, there was a lot of trial and error. There were times when I gave him too much yogurt, and he couldn't tolerate that much dairy or too much sauerkraut, and he had diarrhea. I had a challenging time finding the right bone-to-water ratio to make proper broth and knowing how much to buy to last a week. I also added a few nightshade vegetables to a couple of soup batches that caused inflammatory issues that made him act up. I ran out of broth quite a few times and had to make quick runs to the organic market to buy a chicken just to make some so he would have something to drink with his food. Making sauerkraut was such a time-consuming task that I would always put it off and end up making it right before he ran out, and it wouldn't have the full five days to ferment as it should. I also ended up running out of yogurt a few times, thinking I had a jar left when I didn't. That is not easy to make either because it takes 24 hours for the bacteria to become live.

I was still learning about things from the first stage of the GAPS diet after four months. This experience has strengthened me in many areas like patience, timing, diligence, and balance. All this cooking for Jordan, I also had to make sure others in my family received the same attention. But the most important area I have been strengthened in is peace. Not only with this, but in all areas of my life.

When there is no peace, you can't have happiness. In Lamentations, Jeremiah shared with us the unattractive experiences he had during his trials. He had felt that the Lord's hand was against him, and in the scripture Lamentations 3:17, he says, *"I have been deprived of peace; I have forgotten what prosperity* is" (NIV). There were times when I felt as if I was doing what I was called, yet still not receiving the Lord's grace and mercies. I was bitter, and it showed through a lot of my actions. The diets weren't working as I needed them to, and there were obstacles like receiving unauthorized foods, but I never gave up hope that God would see me through it. I understood that even though things aren't working quite as I want them to, it could always be worse and not work at all.

      It is our job and will be of much comfort to us to be patient for the Lord's salvation. To be patient means to happily and quietly wait. Trial and tribulation are part of the territory to build and shape our character. The issues I was having with the diet allowed me to develop the patience I needed, which gave me peace. And If I could have peace with that, I could have it with everything else. Now we can really get started.

Chapter 9

"Getting stuck"

After being on the GAPS diet for some time, I realized we were still in stage one. It wasn't intentional because, on numerous occasions, I intended to move forward. But every time I introduced something from the second stage, he would have a setback, so I just gave up. Therefore, I didn't get past, giving him soups for breakfast, lunch, and dinner for a while.

The recommendations for stage 2 were to add a raw, organic egg yolk to one bowl of soup until you can work up to one with every bowl. There was also a recipe for a meat casserole I wanted to make using any organic meat I chose. You should keep increasing the amount of sauerkraut and yogurts given at each meal. You can also add stews and casseroles and introduce homemade ghee. The last food you could add was fermented fish. My problem was focusing on only a few of the new foods from this stage, resulting in regression and not trying the other recommendations.

I found this to be like the man who wanted to be healed in John, chapter 5. There was a pool in Jerusalem called Bethesda, where a multitude of sick, lame, paralyzed, and blind people waited. An angel would come down and stir up the waters, and the first step in it would be healed. John 5:5 *"Now a certain man was there who had an infirmity thirty-eight years."* The Message version of the Bible says the man was by the pool for 38 years. Whatever the case was, we know that the man had been there for an extended period. Jesus walked by the pool and asked the man if he wanted to be healed. The man said every time he goes down when the waters are stirred, someone goes in before him. That is the reason why he had been there for so long. I was in a very similar situation. When something unexpected came before me when I tried to move on to the next required step, I didn't move forward and continued to be stuck.

It started with the lamb casserole from stage 2 of the introduction diet. Jordan enjoyed it more than anything I had given him the entire time. However, about the third or fourth time I gave it to him, he showed unruly behaviors while in school again. Initially, when I made it, I used ground spices instead of using herbs. When I did change to use the herbs, it still was an issue. I removed it permanently until I came across information about overeating. I considered that giving him an entire shoulder of lamb may be too much. I attempted it yet again, this time with smaller portions, the only difference was the negative behaviors didn't last as long, but they still appeared. I wasn't, and I am still unsure why he cannot have lamb in this form. He was just fine with it being a soup, so, unfortunately, he could only have it that way and not how he preferred.

The second item I gave him from the second stage was the raw, organic egg yolk in his soup. Adding one was okay, but he didn't respond so well when I increased it to two. I decided to remove it altogether and start it again in a few weeks. I began to give him more sauerkraut and yogurt, but because I did these things simultaneously, I couldn't pinpoint which caused the regression, so I decreased them too.

His doctor suggested a supplement, Collagen Types I & III, to help connective tissues within the body. Connective tissue makes up the outermost part of the digestive tract, and when it becomes inflamed, dysfunction happens. So, I decided to let the supplement have more time to work before moving on to the second stage. But I couldn't stay there.

I realized I had to keep going no matter what obstacles were in my way. Putting away leftovers just in case he was eating our foods or picking at his own was paramount. Once, he ate an entire pot of soup in one day that contained two soup bones, two marrow bones, an oxtail, and two steaks to last him a week and a half. Not only could it have been a source of the problem, but it wasn't cost-effective either.

Going through this made me realize that I can't be idle too long because of one or two issues.

The man who wanted to be healed never got healed by making it to the water because he allowed what was in front of him to stop him. I take away from this verse the man doesn't inch down to be close to his healing when the waters stir, which allowed him to remain there for 38 years. We can't sit in one place because an obstacle jumps in front of us. There are too many options to continue to be stuck. I can't allow things to "jump" in front of me and keep me from moving on.

That's not a good plan or God's plan.

Chapter Ten

"Giving up more"

Several months after the fast was over, I realized that unnecessary things were consuming my time. It was not by television or social media because I had already limited my use of those. This time it was the games I played on my phone instead of being productive. It was time to give it up for a while. It was time for another fast.

I deleted all the games on my phone and vowed not to pick up another PlayStation™ controller until further notice. Both can keep me occupied for hours and hours on end. The time that could be devoted to bettering my relationship with God.

Not long after I decided and went forward with removing them, I started to get more information regarding decisions I was making regarding Jordan and supplements. I wanted to start him because most had been removed and not implemented again because of the diet.

After going over symptoms and behaviors at one of his appointments, the doctor and I both believed that yeast was still a problem within Jordan and why we can't get his behaviors under control. It was decided that we would start him back on the yeast aid, which I had already planned to do when it was right. When I say the time being right, I mean that I hadn't introduced a new food.

Mid-July, I had given the yeast aid supplement to him while we were in the middle of Vacation Bible school. The next day he was not as calm as he had been the previous days. I knew it was the yeast aid because it was the only change that was made.

While observing his behaviors, I decided to see if the GAPS diet helped control yeast over time. That way, I could let the food do its job, and the supplement wouldn't be necessary. At that time, I came across another diet, the Body Ecology Diet (BED), another healing diet. I learned that the GAPS diet does not help remove yeast and even contains foods that can feed it. But recipes within the BED diet help kill off yeast overgrowth and don't allow yeast proliferating foods.

I was taken aback by this new diet I had come across. I wasn't sure if this was God's doing because I started fasting and wasn't distracted by games. When I found I needed to change the foods he ate to help with his behaviors, I was doing the 40-Day Surrender fast.

Was this the I diet I was supposed to be feeding him? Was everything else just a precursor to the one?

It was too early to say. All I could do was research what I had found out and stay still until God directed my next steps. At the end of the week, I purchased the "Body Ecology Diet"[1] book by Donna Gates. I found some helpful information and things I could include from it into the GAPS diet to help with the yeast overgrowth.

To be honest, the thought of a new diet to put Jordan on was unsettling because I felt like I had finally figured out all the ins and outs of the one he was on now. However, this new diet could really be just what he needs to help his organs function how they should and get the nutrients to the right places. I couldn't just jump into it, though. It was going to take some time to know for sure if it was right.

After some consideration, I felt it would be best to stick with the GAPS diet but add a few things from the BED diet to help.

The one that stuck out to me the most to implement was young coconut water kefir. This drink can be made at home and helps control yeast. It also aids in decreasing cravings for sugar, digesting all foods, cleansing the liver that rules the skin, joints, and eyes, giving nicer complexions, easing aches and joint pains and improving vision. It also has superior levels of valuable minerals and just gives you an overall good

---

[1] Gates, Donna. "Body Ecology Diet." Hay House Inc. Carlsbad, CA., (2011)

feeling[2]. I was all for it. It was the first thing I gave him from the BED diet. If I can be honest, I was expecting it to be a "miracle" drink, but not much changed after giving it to him. I did give it to my second youngest daughter, whose PMS symptoms subsided quickly, but that was it.

I had been snapped back into reality because the truth is there is only one miracle worker, and that is the Lord.

I stopped giving him the kefir because it did not do the job, I expected it to do. It also may have been the reason for a slight regression. I should have given it more time to see if it was going to work, but he was in school, and anything that sent him backward was not something I needed to continue to do. I thought about reintroducing it again when school let out. However, since the starter contains yeast and bacteria cultures that go against the protocol he is on, I will not return to it.

It has been months since I have opened a game of Candy Crush™ or Word Cookies™. Not I'm not going to say I don't miss them, but now my mind isn't being occupied at times when I could be praying, having a quiet time with the Lord, and hear Him answer some of the questions I have. And to be clear, I'm not saying that we shouldn't play games and have fun. Most things are okay in moderation. But for me, I wouldn't stop playing a game until all lives were gone, then I would move on to the next until all games were out of lives, then I might check to see if the first game I played had lives replenished.

Even though I am a stay-at-home mom and have idle time, I must make sure my time is used wisely, and I learned that playing games for an hour or more were a misuse of time.

I don't plan to return to playing games, so that means the next time I am ready to fast, God will have to show me something else to give up.

---

[2] Gates, Donna. "Body Ecology Diet." Hay House Inc. Carlsbad, CA., (2011) 125-126

Chapter XI

"The unexpected"

Five months after deciding to fast from games, I still haven't played any mobile games or the PlayStation™, well, maybe the PlayStation once.

Since then, my days have been filled with praying, reading, and meditating. The spiritual journey that I am on is more than just hearing from God about Jordan and his diet. There are many other roles and responsibilities that I have outside of trying to heal his gut.

My most significant part of my life outside of the home was my assistant director position in the Special Needs Ministry (SNM). This included teaching Sunday school, assisting in Bible study, Buddy Break respite care, leading a new parent support group for parents expecting or have a newly diagnosed child with a different ability, creating proposals, and coming up with ideas for ministry meetings.

I unexpectedly returned as an ATF for the DDS Ministry, which required a lot of studying, focus, commitment, and attention for ten months. I had added gymnastics to my daughter's schedule that I saw her, too, as well as caring for a friend's children and helping with homework after school. The latter of 2017 had been one for the memory books and didn't look like it would slow down.

I hadn't planned on being a part of the DDS ministry that season. That was because when it was time to sign up, the SNM had just been awarded a house owned by the church to serve as the new host site for the Buddy Break respite care. A lot of preparation had to be put into place to get it up to code. Then it would need to be fixed up to provide a video room, sensory room, and fine and gross motor rooms, all while having enough space to provide for the growing number of children whose parents wanted them to attend. The benefit of having the house was it was strictly for our use. With our church's permission, we could schedule anytime, and for however long we liked. The problem with the house was its size, location, and parking. Since it just wasn't right, we declined the place. Doing this afforded me the free time needed to continue to serve in DDS.

However, I still hadn't planned on going back, but while at the ladies' graduation in my first class, I learned there was a shortage of ATF's or assistants to the facilitators. I had to pray on serving again because I was without a vehicle and already had other obligations that I had signed up for and using my mother's car to do them. I had agreed to come back after she said I could use it. But since I have gotten a new car. Praise God!

One of the requirements for returning and new ATF's was reading a book called "God's Armor Bearers."[1] There are many different examples given in the Bible regarding armor-bearers. The most significant role, in my opinion, was the one David had to King Saul in the book of 1 Samuel.

Saul was troubled. His servants saw how distressed he was and sought to find someone who could play the harp, so when he was down, the music would make him feel well. Jesse's son David, who was also anointed by God to be King over Israel, was brought to Saul, and he loved him, and he became his armorbearer.

Goliath, a Philistine, came forth with a challenge to the Israelites that if a man of their choosing were to kill him, the Philistines would be their slaves, and if Goliath killed their soldier, the Israelites would be slaves to the Philistines. David came forth and killed Goliath, but Saul became angry when they returned home from battle, and the women from the cities came out singing and dancing, saying, *"Saul has slain his thousands, and David his ten thousands" (1 Sam. 18:7).*

Saul sought to kill David, but he escaped and departed from him. Saul was given into David's hand, but he chose not to take his life because he was still his master. David was the definition of a true armorbearer.

[1] Nance, Terry. "God's Armor Bearer, Volumes 1&2". Focus on the Harvest, Inc. Sherwood, AR., (1990)

Although I don't think I will ever be in a position where someone in authority over me would choose to end my life, I want to serve all those I am under in such a manner. My husband, my director, and my facilitator should always feel supported by me in every avenue they face. And after reading the book, I realized I hadn't been as supportive as I should have been of my husband, and I saw I wasn't meeting the needs of my director as well as I could have been.

Being an armorbearer isn't an easy thing to do because you must be obedient to who you serve, regardless of how you feel about the situation. You will not see eye to eye on all things, but you are to follow their lead if it isn't illegal, immoral, or unethical. It has been a bit of a struggle holding my tongue, but it also has its benefits. I noticed the times when I said nothing and followed my husband's lead; God allowed him to see things my way.

Handling things in this manner dealing with my husband gave me peace that I had never had before. That peace has carried over to the behavior issues with Jordan. I was no so concerned when Jordan had an off day at school as I had been in times past because learning what an armorbearer should do taught me another level to being obedient, which gave me that peace. And we all know that scripture says to obey is better than sacrifice.

Chapter 12

"Finding the root of it all"

When we ask God to intervene in the storms of our lives, we usually ask for the rain to stop. But if there was no rain and only wind, a lot of damage could still be done.

The definition of wind is uneven heating of the earth's surface by the sun. Unbalance usually causes storms in our lives, and the wind would be the leading cause of the harm done.

Now, have you ever taken notice of how many times God references wind in the Bible? At the time of writing this, I had been directed to 2 of them. In the book Matthew, Jesus and his disciples went on a boat to go to the other side. *Matthew 14:24 says, "But the boat was now in the middle of the sea, tossed by the waves, for the wind was contrary."* In Mark 4, again, Jesus is in a boat, this time with the others crossing over to the other side. This time he was in the stern asleep and was awakened by them because of waves crashing against and water filling the boat. Mark 4:39 says, *"Then He arose and rebuked the wind and said to the sea, 'Peace, be still!' And the wind ceased, and there was a great calm."*

In both scriptures, the wind is the cause of waves hitting the boats because it's what stir up the waters. The root of it all. Rain and clouds aren't the real problems behind storms. It's the wind that damages trees, knocks down power lines, rips roofs off homes, and causes the water to make boats capsize.

For years I have been trying to address the causes for Jordan's behavior that may come from having allergic reactions to foods and the environment, developmental delay, and a weak immune system.

Even though autism is classified as a neurological issue or a brain disorder because the symptoms are one of a damaged brain, the cause for it has been described as a three-faceted illness with direct damage to the immune system, the gastrointestinal system, and the nervous system[1]. That is, according to Dr. Kenneth Bock, M.D. Until we fix these systems issues, we will never fully know if the brain can work as it should work in children with autism and, therefore, remove the diagnosis.

I remember praying to God to heal him and make him "normal" as my other children. Essentially, I asked for the symptoms to be removed and not wanting to know the root of why he had them in the first place. But those requests went unanswered because I wasn't asking for the right thing. *James 4:3, "You ask and do not receive, because you ask amiss, that you may spend it on your pleasures."* Once I began getting my vertical relationship with God in order, He started to show me what I needed to address and how.

For example, the problem I had in detoxifying him. If the body is deficient in iron, it will be hard to remove lead because their properties are very similar. He was also eating some of his foods out of ceramic bowls where the glaze contains lead. When I started praying more and reading the word, it led me to this information. I began using different bowls and started him on an iron supplement, and his lead level changed. It helped me get to the source and showed me how fasting works.

Back in 2013, I learned one of the reasons to fast is to gain spiritual rewards. A few of them are **discernment** (Acts 14:23), **direction** (Judges 20:26-28), **humility** (Psalm 35:13), **answered prayers** (2 Samuel 12:15-16), and finally, **healing** (Mark 9:29)[2].

Today I think back to when I first started to fast. I started by turning down my plate the Saturday I collected urine for testing. Later I realized that wasn't going to be helpful because we had already gone through the chelation process. I then decided to fast from eating on the

---

[1] Bock M.D., Kenneth & Stauth, Cameron. "Healing the New Childhood Epidemics: Autism, ADHD, Asthma, and Allergies." Ballentine Books, New York (2007) 82
[2] Jenkins., John K. "Fasting" First Baptise Church of Glenarden Bible Study, Upper Marlboro, MD (April 16, 2013)

weekends of chelation. From Friday at about 3 p.m. until Monday at 3 a.m., I wouldn't eat anything. I did this in hopes that the lead levels would have had a significant decline.

The way that I went about fasting all wrong. I was trying to force God to do something for me. But we need to fast for biblical reasons, not our own. God wasn't going to honor things done in such a selfish matter.

Even though it is the way you should do it, according to the bible, it wouldn't be beneficial for me to fast from eating because there were plenty of times where I was saddened and wouldn't eat for days. So, this wasn't something that showed God I was giving up something for Him.

The 40-Day Surrender Fast came just in time. Preparing for it taught me the true meaning of fasting and how to do it correctly. Now that I had a better understanding, I could receive what I needed to get from it.

Fasting has become my way of getting answers. I saw significant improvements in Jordan after fasting the two times I did and implemented what I had learned. Now, I think back to the verses of Mark chapter 1 that talked about Jesus casting out an unclean spirit and in chapter 9 as below.

***

> [17] Then one of the crowd answered and said, "Teacher, I brought You my son, who has a mute spirit. [18] And wherever it seizes him, it throws him down; he foams at the mouth, gnashes his teeth, and becomes rigid. So I spoke to Your disciples, that they should cast it out, but they could not." [19] He answered him and said, "O faithless generation, how long shall I be with you? How long shall I bear with you? Bring him to Me." [20] Then they brought him to Him. And when he saw Him, immediately the spirit convulsed him, and he fell on the ground and wallowed, foaming at the mouth. [21] So He asked his father, "How long has this been happening to him?" And he said, "From childhood. [22] And often he has thrown him both into the fire and into the water to destroy him. But if You can do

anything, have compassion on us and help us." ²³ Jesus said to him, "If you can believe, all things are possible to him who believes." ²⁴ Immediately the father of the child cried out and said with tears, "Lord, I believe; help my unbelief!" ²⁵ When Jesus saw that the people came running together, He rebuked the unclean spirit, saying to it: "Deaf and dumb spirit, I command you, come out of him and enter him no more!" ²⁶ Then the spirit cried out, convulsed him greatly, and came out of him. And he became as one dead, so that many said, "He is dead." ²⁷ But Jesus took him by the hand and lifted him privately, "Why could we not cast it out?" ²⁹ So He said to them, "This kind can come out by nothing but prayer and fasting."

***

Chapter Thirteen

"Something new"

One of the things that I have acquired since having a child with a special need is stress. I'm sure that's not much of a surprise. However, what has come of the pressure may be.

Over the years since his diagnosis, I have developed trichotillomania, which is the pulling out of hair, which kept getting worse the more I would add to my plate with Jordan and treatment.

During the 40-day surrender fast, attempting to not pull at my eyelashes, which was my go-to, was something I wanted to focus on as well. I was successful in not doing so, but I couldn't help but go back to it after the fast was over. I mean, I could have, but because it wasn't something I was doing for God, it wasn't something that I felt I had to abstain from, and therefore it became a habit again.

After returning to DDS, I had a new prayer partner the ministry assigned me to. Our first prayer session was on a Monday, and we didn't decide if it was going to be an everyday thing or once or twice a week. After conferring and agreeing to do it twice a week, we also decided to incorporate fasting. Since I started making better choices when it came to how I ate, I felt like I could now turn down my plate for a brief time to not revert to my old way of eating, and it would be more meaningful than in times past.

Yet, I still want to work on my other bad habit to feel like I look like a normal human being. I'm not sure if others notice it, but it's uncomfortable for me to walk around with my lashes as jacked up as they are. I know there are remedies to the problem, such as buying false ones, but it's really a hassle to put them on daily, and it's only covering the symptom, not a solution to the problem. Therefore, I had decided to fast on it yet again. And every day, think of it as so, so that I can stop altogether.

I don't speak on it much, but it is a part of my journey that I try to be transparent about, so I felt the need to share it. Since starting this new fast, I began to receive more confirmations from God.

In October 2017, Jordan had another visit with his DAN! Doctor. In the past, when looking at the take-home instructions toward the end, I hardly ever second-guessed if God approved what she recommended. Eventually, I started praying on it, but it was more of a formality, to be honest with you. I would act as if I was praying for His guidance, but realistically my mind was already made up to do it before leaving the office.

Typically, before a follow-up, I would have an idea on what course of treatment I would like to try the next couple of months, but this day I had no suggestions on what I feel should be the next "thing." So, it was all up to the doctor this time. Because of that, I made a conscious decision that I would have to pray long and hard before I implemented what she said because I need to make sure it is part of God's will for his treatment.

Observations I shared about Jordan with her were that his behavior pattern was still unpredictable, although he didn't act up often. One cause could have been that there was the yeast problem that I thought was somewhat getting under control.

But I couldn't help but feel like there was an unknown source. Mainly because one day, out of the blue, he asked me to cook his onions in the olive oil that I used to make them in. I had switched to ghee because when I first started making his eggs in them, he gave me the impression he really liked it, plus I thought it would be more fattening since I was trying to get him to put on more weight. Usually, I would put down something like this as an observation, but it never made it to the list.

After processing all the information I gave her, she suggested the Nemechek Protocol (NP). This addresses SIBO, small intestine bacterial overgrowth. This procedure includes adding **olive oil** to meals and cooking. This was my confirmation from God.

Because I had not found the NP before and had time to research, I now had to go home and do so.

Some of the requirements Dr. Nemechek, the NP's creator, have for going on the protocol varied from what Jordan's doctor prescribed. Coming off probiotics and adding inulin and EPA/DHA was the same, but he says to come off enzymes as well, while she said it was up to me. Also, to stop taking any antifungals, whereas she told me to continue with all current supplements. Lastly, for this procedure, you don't have to be on any kind of diet. My, I wish she agreed with that for Jordan. But she calls for me to stay following the GAPS/BED diets.

There was only one thing to do at that point. Gather all information I can about NP by purchasing The Nemechek Protocol for Autism and Developmental Disorders[1]. Once I was done getting everything I could from man, I would ask for direction from God.

---

[1] Nemecheck, D.O., Patrick M. "The Nemechek Protocol™: For Autism and Developmental Disorders." San Bernardino, CA (2017)

Chapter xiv

"From having doubt to getting clarity"

After gathering everything I needed to know before starting Jordan on the Nemechek Protocol and still fasting from pulling my eyelashes, I had mixed emotions about everything moving forward and everything that I had done in the past.

I came across another book, yet again, telling me that what they have discovered can reverse autism.

First, there was "Healing the New Childhood Epidemics" that talked about diets and supplements that helped change the effects of autism.

After that, I read "The Un-Prescription for Autism," which talked about different diets and supplements and expressed the need for certain bacteria to be in place in high dosages.

Then there was "The Gut and Psychology Syndrome," which said the gut had to be healed to start the recovery process. The one after that was the "Body Ecology Diet" that explained how this is the diet to heal by focusing on proper food combining, eliminating yeast proliferating foods, and various other principles, too many to name.

Now, this "Nemechek Protocol" explains a bacterial overgrowth that needs to be addressed so microglia can do the job it's supposed to do in repairing the brain. To be honest, I didn't know what to think anymore.

Being armed with all the information I had read over the years, it was tough to believe that this would be the one. The one that will give my son the ability to converse with me. The one that will allow him to learn the way his typical peers do. The one that will be able to remove the label of autism from my son.

All the recommendations the books gave I implemented: removing gluten, adding supplements, taking away foods that have artificial flavors and colors out of his diet, and getting rid of the foods that contain a natural ingredient that is problematic to some. The last thing I did was change his diet to give meals and broths that can help heal a permeated gut so toxins can't leak into the body and get nutrients where they are supposed to go, especially the brain. Now I must add another supplement that will help control a bacteria overgrowth within his small intestine. Seems like I have been here before, and it didn't yield the results I thought it would. What makes this one any different?

You can only tell a person so many times that treatment is going to work, and when it doesn't, find another one that says it will work and continue to believe there is something out there that will do what it says it will.

It's only human nature to start having doubts when you continue to read books that keep feeding you the same stories about those whose children were recovered doing this, but yours hasn't. It makes you wonder if it's all just a big hoax to give parents false hope about their child's diagnosis being able to be changed.

I was starting to feel that way. Part of me wants to just give up because I can't keep going through the struggles of changing diets and regimens to have Jordan improve slightly, but in the end, I still have the same problems he was faced with at the beginning. It's too hard to bear.

Luckily, I remembered I serve a God who, through Him, anything is possible. This way of viewing our situation is one of putting my trust in man.

Humans wrote these books. Now I'm not saying they aren't God-inspired, but if one has the remedy to heal, and the other does but goes about another way of doing it, doesn't it seem to contradict? I mean, it may be possible that you could heal a child with either or, but it tends to make you a little leery about the accuracy of them all. Let me give you an example of what I mean:

In "Healing the New Childhood Epidemics," Dr. Bock recalls some cases where he has children presented with the typical symptoms of autism. His healing program consisted of four components. They are **nutritional therapy:** whole, organic and nutrient-dense foods, removing allergenic and yeast proliferating foods, gluten/casein-free diet if necessary and limited carbohydrates for some. **Supplementation therapy:** supplements that detox, support the metabolism and brain, energize, kill fungi as well as parasites and bacteria. **Detoxification:** includes chelation and methylation and stimulates the organs that detoxify and eliminate toxins. And then **medications:** they can range from antifungals, antibiotics, antivirals, and anti-inflammatories. He does go on to say, "there is no single magic bullet for any of the disorders."

After rereading some of the books, I realized where I went wrong. I focused on one area, and the other regions became neglected and spiraled out of control. The books that followed showed me what the first book told me, but I failed to address each issue and only focused on the apparent ones.

Following the directions of "man" only and not including God in the treatment was one of my biggest mistakes. I had to address issues that I wouldn't have needed because I left Him out of the program.

It took fasting and a little doubt to make me realize that not including Him to hear what He had to say about it played a significant role in why things are like they are. But now that I have clarity where there was doubt, I will not make the same mistakes again.

---

[1]Bock, M.D., Kenneth & Stauth, Cameron. "Healing the New Childhood Epidemics: Autism, ADHD, Asthma, and Allergies." Ballentine Books, New York (2007) 22-25

Chapter 15

"Learning patience"

As I shared in the last chapter, I had a little doubt about if this new protocol would be the one that would do everything that I needed it to do, and therefore, I asked myself the question, "Would I continue on with treatment if this didn't work out?"

I debated this for days because I just couldn't imagine getting my hopes up time after time, and the result is the same as it had been for the last 7-8 years. Then God told me to think about Abraham.

In the book of Genesis, when he was still called Abram, God told him to get out of his country to a land He will show him. At that time, he was 75 years old. God told him on various occasions that the land He will give him will go to his descendants. Finally, Abram spoke to the Lord regarding His promises a few chapters later. *Genesis 15:2-3: ₂"But Abram said, 'Lord God, what will You give me, seeing I go childless, and the heir of my house is Eliezer of Damascus?' ₃ Then Abram said, 'Look, You have given me no offspring; indeed one born in my house is my heir!'"* The Lord responded to him that the heir would come from his own body. Remember, he was 75 years old.

Because Sarai, now called Sarah, was barren, she gave her maidservant to Abraham to bear him children. She and Abraham had not been able to conceive, and because the Lord said he was going to have a descendant, she took matters into her own hands. Abraham was 86 years old when Hagar, the maidservant, bore Ishmael. However, the Lord told Abraham that Sarah, although she was well past childbearing years, would give him a son named Isaac. Because of Abraham's obedience to the Lord when he told him to leave his father's house, he kept the covenant He made with him, and Sarah bore Isaac to him at the age of 90. And

Abraham was 100 years of age. It took 25 years for God to honor the promise He made with Abraham, but He held true to His word.

In *Mark 9:29*, God said some things can only come out through prayer and fasting. The scripture was about a child who was mute and had seizures. Although Jordan is not entirely speechless and does not have seizures, I relate his condition to the boys. Therefore, I believe that what God's word says is true and that this can be removed through prayer and fasting.

I have been treating Jordan holistically since 2009; he was five years old. It has been nine years that I have been expecting something miraculous to happen that took God 25 years to do for Abraham. I want Jordan to be typical within a few months of a new supplement when it took 40 years for God to bring the children of Israel into the promised land. What makes me so unique that I should receive His promise to me in a few years?

Even though God didn't make this promise directly to me, His word is always true. When God's hand was with his people at war, He gave the enemy into their hands. And when the enemy sought after those who obeyed Him, He gave them protection, so they were not harmed. The multitudes who followed Him and had no food, He provided food for them. So, when He gives us numerous examples in the bible on how He is a healer, we must believe.

There is not anything that God cannot do, and circumstance is higher than His ability to handle. Jordan is no exception. Therefore, I will not stop. It took the children 40 years to reach the promised land because of their inability to fully trust God. My life is no exception. I take matters into my own hands plenty of times because I don't want to wait. Or I put my trust in man's word instead of the Lord's. This journey is going to take some time because I will continue to fall short. But I will be patient because my reward, whatever it is, will be great.

Chapter 16

"Improvement"

Over the last nine years, I have seen many improvements with Jordan.

Due to the gluten-free diet, he started to sleep through the night. Initiating chelation and supplements increased his eye contact, gave more speech, and the types of foods he would eat. I was thrilled at the strides he was making, but we still had issues in other areas like retaining what he learned in school, echolalia, focusing, and of course, his behaviors.

For a while, we seemed to be at a standstill. Trying to find the right combination of supplements to keep Jordan obedient was very difficult to do. But that's not what I want to talk about in this chapter.

When I incorporated fasting into my walk with Christ, as the book's subtitle says, it changed everything. *Psalm 35:13, "But as for me, when they were sick, My clothing was sackcloth; I humbled myself with fasting; And my prayer would return to my own heart."* I had to learn to be humble and deny some of my desires. And doing so, I was shown what God wanted me to do regarding Jordan and treatment. That was when I saw Jordan had significant growth.

Implementing the NP was from where that growth came. I started to see his focus grow. I already knew he liked to color, but when I gave him a new coloring book, he worked on it the entire day and only stopped when he needed to eat or use the bathroom. He started to ask for things I have never heard him ask for and asked for them appropriately. He was also answering questions I asked him instead of repeating what I said. I think back to a time where he told me something was hurting him. I asked him what happened, and he responded with "fall." I followed up and asked him at school or home, in that order, and he said school. He voiced his want to leave the auto dealership with the oil changes was taking too long for him. He needed less prompting to tell you sorry or bless you, and he had put on some weight. He went from 87 to 104 pounds, where he stayed for some time. I could go on and on with the list of advancements I saw in him, but I'll stop here and say I was delighted with what I saw him do on the Nemechek Protocol™. I was concerned if it would help resolve anything, but I should have known better than to doubt something God confirmed to me.

There was a bit of a problem while on the protocol, though. Jordan's behaviors never improved. I still received notes, I had to pick him up just as much as before, and many times because of that, I kept him home. I was confused as to how he could show much improvement in one area but not the other. It wasn't until I came across a question asked by another parent using the protocol that caused me to look deeper into histamine.

The entire time Jordan had been going through treatment, he took fish oil. It started out with cod liver oil, and after so many ears went by, switching to a fermented cod liver oil. From there, we had to start him on the EPA/EHA omega 3 oil for the NP.

He had been skin tested for allergies back when he was first diagnosed and showed to be allergic to shellfish and seafood. But I continued to give him these oils.

When he was younger, I never physically saw his intolerance. But as time went on, I'm assuming it started to become a problem. That's because after I put the two together and his doctor told me to remove it and put him on an antihistamine diet, his behavior started to improve. I only had to remove the avocado I gave him with breakfast.

After a few days, there were no more calls home from school. The notes stopped coming in the agenda book about kicking chairs or throwing things at classmates. The last few weeks of school were terrific. I noticed a minor setback when I tried to add a vegan brand of the oil, but once I discontinued it, he went right back to being behaved.

I wasn't receiving any adverse reports from his school; however, I still liked to base things on what I saw. I evaluated how things affect him by observing him at Bible study or our Buddy Break respite care.

Even though I serve, I allow him to attend to get out of the house, interact with other children, and get a lesson. His behaviors at the last Buddy break he attended had me in awe. For the most part, he sat with his buddy and colored. But his whole demeanor was different.

When it was time for lunch, he stopped coloring and looked for his lunch bag, and when I told him it was already in the snack room, he proceeded to go there. While eating the soup he had due to his strict diet, he did not ask for the other children's other snacks like he usually did. During lesson time, he turned and listened intently.

After the lesson was over, he did ask for a bag of chips. I felt because he did such an excellent job the entire day, I could give him one. After one, he usually annoys me for another. But when I returned to take him back to his assigned room, he picked up his trash and followed without asking for a second. That was indeed a fantastic day.

After all the things I had been through, it felt good to finish this book with a list of positive things I saw in Jordan.

By the time you read this, I will have a longer list of achievements seen in Jordan due to the protocol and hearing from God what to do when a setback occurs. But for now, relish knowing that fasting is a vital part of your walk with God. It led me to hear Him, follow the directions set before, and see the remarkable things I see in Jordan today. Imagine if you did the same and the outcome you could see in your situations.

Do it and thank me later.

Chapter Seventeen

"Time to be quiet"

For years I have tried to be as transparent as I could about everything in my life as it revolves around autism and not just the treatment.

I believe there are many out there like me that are going through the same kinds of challenges. Whether you want to treat health issues holistically, marital or financial problems, or whatever. I've learned and grown so much that it would be against God's word not to share the knowledge I have gained and the testimonies I have had so that it could help someone else. *Hebrews 13:16, "But do not forget to do good and to share, for with such sacrifices God is well pleased."*

Through my blog and ministry meetings, I have shared so much about things Jordan had to overcome and his regressions. If you are a follower of my blog, you've seen I have shared about food, nutrition, supplements, diets, blood test results, and the embarrassment of urination habits. I've spoken about problems within my marriage and financial burdens relating to autism. You have also been a witness to many breakthroughs and crossing difficult hurdles.

I have been an open book to some degree, and you have seen much of my highs and lows.

There are a lot of things I do keep private. Most of my personal life outside autism is off-limits. I don't speak much about my children unless it relates to how Jordan has interacted with them. I don't share the date night we have because I feel we must have some things to ourselves. It Is the main reason why my Facebook™ page is dry. If we aren't close enough to share my life with you in person, you will not find anything I do in a post or picture. My life is just that my life.

Since September of 2017, I have shared a lot about fasting. It has been a massive part of my testimony because God moved once it became a regular part of my routine. Plus, I try to live by *Psalm 22:22, "I will praise you to all my brothers; I will stand before the congregation and testify of the wonderful things you have done." (TLB).* It wouldn't be right if I shared with you all the good but not what happened to get there. I had to inform you of the times where I fasted to give you the whole picture. But it's not an easy thing to do.

I say this because *Matthew 6:5-6 says, $_5$ "And when you pray, you shall not be like the hypocrites. For they love to pray standing in the synagogues and on the corners of the streets, that they may be seen by men. Assuredly, I say to you, they have their reward, $_6$ But you, when you pray, go into your room, and when you have shut your door, pray to your Father who is in the secret place; and your Father who sees in secret will reward you openly."* It's very conflicting to speak on things I believe should be done in private. However, I don't think I could have shared my story without it. It is the reason why I consider myself to have a lot of positive outcomes, and not all related to autism.

I don't know what my life would be without fasting the right way. It caused me to remove many dead things in my life that weren't doing anything to benefit the kingdom of God. Because of eliminating television, I had more time to read and catch up on a year's worth of bible studies that helped me revitalize my marriage and have a better relationship with my children.

Pastor John K. Jenkins Sr., my pastor, did a series on relationships that helped me accomplish that. I received a new understanding of handling finances and being content with what I had instead of always looking to get more.

I also started making better decisions on how I spent my time and what I fed my spirit with when it came to TV shows, movies I watched, and what I saw on social media. Overall, fasting gave me a sense of peace in my life that I don't think I would have otherwise had.

I came to grips that I no longer had to worry about certain things, like if there would be enough money to cover everything I needed to for the week.

I stopped putting expectations in my husband to be the man I wanted him to be instead of the man he is, and therefore it made me stop looking down on who he was.

And most importantly, I stopped having anxiety when I would receive a note home about Jordan's behaviors at school before the changes. The situations may not be ideal, but to overextend myself trying to figure out how I would handle it, was not my8 place.

I had to trust the Lord that we would make it through the week financially, that my husband was a great man, and I can't be a source of stress to him.

Most of all, it made me see that Jordan's behaviors were an indication that I needed to do something more, and God's not done with s yet.

I'm thankful to share what fasting has done for me and give you a glimpse of what it can do. And if God can do it for me, He can do it for you.

However, because there are some things we aren't supposed to broadcast for others to see, my time talking about fasting has come to an end. It will continue to be prominent in my life, but now it will be between God and me. The way it should be.

Chapter XVII

"Other POV's"

On occasion, I ask my husband if he has noticed any differences in Jordan's behaviors after starting a new supplement or food because I need another perspective.

I am not the only person around Jordan, and sometimes I need to know if someone caught something I missed. Also, because Jordan is a different person when around his dad than he is when around me, and there may be somethings that he sees that I won't.

Therefore, I wanted to do something different and allow him to share with others about how it feels to be raising a son with autism. After bringing the idea to him, he was on board and agreed to contribute a few words.

I won't get into the details of what his chapter may consist of because, honestly, I don't know what he's going to say. But I am looking forward to reading whatever he has to say to better understand his relationship with Jordan and maybe be more compassionate about his feelings about having a son with special needs.

After getting a yes from him, I thought I could go a step further and include my other children.

I have four girls, three older and one younger than Jordan, who have opinions and feelings regarding having a brother who sometimes acts like any other younger/older brother may, but has a different reason why he does the things he does.

First, I asked my 17-year-old at the time if she wanted to write a chapter because she was the one who at one time felt Jordan did the things he did to her to get on her nerves. After paying attention to what she had told me, I think she may have been on to something with that theory.

Next, I asked my oldest biologically who was home from Morgan for the holidays. She and Jordan have a unique relationship. When he isn't entirely out of control, she can get him to do things others in the home can't, and she can teach him in a way that he listens. She also agreed to share her side. Three down, two to go.

I asked my stepdaughter, the oldest of all the kids in the home, if she would like to share something regarding her relationship with Jordan. Her response was typical of her; it didn't matter. I just told her to let me know if she wanted to or not and left it at that.

I sat down with my 8-year-old to ask her if she wanted to. Of all the girls, she is closest to him because, chronologically, they were the same age at one point. Even though he annoys her at times, she is protective of him and engages with him. When they both had tablets, and he played Temple Run™, she would get hers, and they would play simultaneously. She also loved to skate around the house with him. They have a unique bond. She was happy I asked her and agreed to share her experience of having Jordan as her older brother.

Later that night, my mother came home to help with some of the Thanksgiving cooking. I spoke with her about my long night working on the book and creating the cover. It was then I realized she was a grandmother of a child with autism. I extended the invitation to share her experiences in a chapter as well. She was willing to do so with a bit of help getting what she wanted to say across.

That was a yes from 5 out of 6. I wish I could have a Jordan piece. I often wonder what he thinks about if he notices the difference between himself and everyone else in the house. If things go the right way, maybe by the next book. I speak it in the air and claim it!

Without further delay, here are chapters from the most essential people in Jordan's life. Donald (Daddy), Damecia-Tionne (Tiaah), Sierra (SiSi), Kaiyah (Kaiyah), and Loretta (Guammah). (The names in parentheses are how he pronounces their names.)

Chapter Nineteen

"Daddy"

July 18, 2004. That was the day, the day my son was born. Although he was not my first child, he was my first and only boy.

The first few years were typical to me; my wife saw things differently. Around year 3 was when she knew something wasn't quite right. We talked about it extensively, but I believed things were moving slow and that he will do everything, just in his own time. My wife was sure her gut was right.

Right before he was to turn 4, she had him evaluated, and her feeling was right. Autism was his diagnosis. The struggle was about to begin.

I, we, had no idea what was ahead of us. Even after the official diagnosis, I still had a tough time accepting it. "Not my son; he will be just fine," is what I continuously told myself.

But as time passed, I began to realize what autism was and how it affects each person differently. It also occurred to me that many of the things that I envisioned us doing, you know, father and son things, would not happen.

That was particularly hard for me. There would be no battles on the football or baseball field or the basketball court. Instead, my son would struggle with things that most people don't ever think twice about doing. My battle was trying to understand what he wants and fights to do. Many simple things we do in everyday life.

I had to learn to be patient all over again because dealing with a child of this nature requires a different kind of patience. After getting the diagnosis, my wife, on the other hand, began her journey. She started reading and researching, trying to find whatever she could about autism and life after learning your child has this disorder.

Through her findings, she began to teach me. As I learned more about autism. I understood a lot of what made Jordan, Jordan. However, my biggest obstacle is learning to live in his world and understand how he processes information. It's a little tricky because just when I think I'm beginning to understand, things change.

It has been a long, trying road to get where we are right now. But today, I have hope. The things that are being done by my wife to give Jordan a better quality of life have given me faith. The things I thought I would never be able to do with him, I believe one day I will. That is because he is doing things I didn't think I would get to see him do. He participated in the Special Olympics, showing interest in cars and even interacting with me occasionally. Every day I see more changes in him due to his diet and supplements to recover. All this came about after my wife read one Bible verse.

Mark 9:29, "So He said to them, 'This kind can come out by nothing but prayer and fasting.'" It is her favorite scripture in the Bible. The verse gave her the strength to keep going when things didn't look well with treatment. It showed her that amid praying, she also had to fast. When she learned something while fasting and applied it to Jordan's regimen, he progressed.

That is a prime example of how God's word is true. So, just like my wife, I also believe that my son can recover. I am now looking forward to those sports battles and moments that only a father and son can share.

Chapter 20

"Tiaah Q&A"

Ever since I decided to implement everyone's outlook in the book, I have been pressing my oldest to complete her chapter.

When she came home for Christmas break, I just knew she would be focused enough to complete it. However, on her fourth day home, after asking her about it for maybe the 50th time, she said she wanted to forgo her input because she didn't know what to say.

When I offered for Kaiyah to give her input, I asked her how she felt about her brother instead of writing something because she was only 8. Her responses weren't quite what I was looking for, so I gave her specific questions to answer. Because Tionne was having difficulty in what to say, I afforded her the same opportunity. I asked her the questions before I sat down with Kaiyah to do hers, so hers appears first.

So here is Tionne, my now 21-year-old's outlook on having Jordan as a brother.

Me: Do you remember when Jordan was diagnosed with autism when you were the age of 8?

T: Yes. Well, I didn't know for sure what autism was, but I knew there was something wrong. I remember I had a special handshake with him, and before we went on one vacation we went on, he didn't do it anymore. But later he started to do it with me again.

Me: Do you remember us explaining autism to you?

T: No. I only remember us getting in trouble for saying the r-word and writing a paper on it.

Me: Do you remember when you found out the definition of autism?

T: Yeah. I remember learning about it from a TV show in which a kid had Asperger's. I don't remember you explaining to me what autism was.

Me: Okay. Let's talk about Jordan. How did you feel once you learned what autism was and seeing Jordan's symptoms and then put the two together that's what he had?

T: I felt like I couldn't play fight with my brother the way sisters fight with their brothers. I am still upset about that.

Me: Were you concerned about Jordan and his future?

T: No, I figured he would grow out of it.

Me: How did you feel growing up with a brother that had a disability?

T: I felt extremely protective.

Me: Elaborate more, please.

T: I felt protective of him because of the disability. And it expanded to being defensive and sympathetic to all children with disabilities.

Me: What is the hardest thing to deal with due to him having autism?

T: Not knowing how to help him when he needs help. Like the earache that he kept telling me about yesterday. I could do nothing to help him, but it was clear he wanted me to do something about it, and I believe he thought I didn't understand him because he kept asking.

Me: Did you feel there was favoritism when it came to me and Jordan?

T: Yeah, there still is. I also felt like there would be favoritism if he didn't have autism because he was the only boy.

Me: Knowing what you know about Jordan, and autism, do you wish that he was just like everybody else?

T: I feel like he's faking on not talking. I feel like he does it to get away with certain things. Unfortunately, it backfires because he can't have pizza.

Me: You don't honestly believe that do you?

T: No. But I do believe he knows what he's doing and can't communicate properly.

Me: So, do you wish he was like everyone else?

T: No, because his autism makes him funnier than I think he would be if he didn't have autism. I remember when he threw deodorant at Sierra, one of the most fun days living on earth. He was being nothing but honest, but it was funny.

Me: So, what happened that day?

T: SiSi did something to irritate him. So, he went upstairs to her room, got her deodorant off her shelf, and came back downstairs to the den and threw it at her. The kid is just funny, and I love his personality.

Me: Last question? Do you agree with the path I am taking to heal him to potentially be like everyone else?

T: Yeah. Because at the same time, he must learn how to take care of himself. If something were to happen, he wouldn't know what to do. But I believe if he were to learn sign language to communicate and he would be somewhat okay.

Chapter Twenty-one

"SiSi"

Sierra is Jordan's 18-year-old sister.

Before I share her side of having a brother with special needs, I wanted to give a little background on her. Sierra is my second-born daughter.

When she was younger, she also suffered some of the side effects of living in a basement that had mold. One day after dropping her off at daycare, I was called to pick her up because she showed signs of pink eye in both eyes.

Sierra is a little immature for her age. As she progressed into middle and high school, I saw she had a challenging time with socialization. To me, she had an awkwardness about her.

In 2015 I learned there was a possibility she had Asperger's. I never had her evaluated because I couldn't bear to have that label put on her. She has a tough time remembering to do all her chores, which I think is a lack of focus because it does not interest her. When she is around the house most times, she always seems to be down and depressed.

To change her perspective on life, I had to change myself. I had to enter her world to view things the way she did, and it helped our relationship, and I believe it proved to her that I do care about and love her.

I still feel that Asperger's is apparent, but that's another child, another book.

Here is her outlook on having a brother with autism.

***

"SiSi"

Jordan...oh man. Where do I even begin with this one?

He is usually a very complicated person to deal with and live with. Sometimes he is nice, and other times he's funny. But most of the time, his misbehavior is far beyond annoying. Don't get me wrong, he is my brother, and I love him, but a lot of the things he does are, how should I put this, questionable. It's not like any of that previous information matters; the only real explanation that can explain it is that he indeed has autism and usually cannot control his actions. Not that any of that is a terrible thing. I generally enjoy his presence; that is when he isn't upset.

My mom seems to show a lot of favoritism towards him, and I believe it's because he's the only boy she gave birth to and because he has autism. She buys him a lot of electronics and almost gave him an entire laptop and one point. He also used to be the only one with a TV in his room and had both Wii™ systems we had given to him as well, even though he wasn't the only one that played them. She also gives him plenty of love and attention and is much more patient with him than with the rest of us. My older sisters and I see it as favoritism, but my mom as loving her son. It may be one or the other, or even both. Who knows? All I know is our mom loves her son very much.

***

Chapter XXII

"Kaiyah Q&A"

When talking to Kaiyah about what she wanted to say in her chapter, the only thing she kept saying is how much she loved her brother.

However, I needed to get other kinds of information from her. So, I ended up asking her questions about how she felt having a brother with special needs. It led me to change up her chapter to do a question-and-answer section just for her.

Me: Introduce yourself to our readers.

Kaiyah: My name is Kaiyah, and I am Jordan's little sister.

Me: How does it feel to have a brother with special needs who can't talk like the rest of us?

K: I feel sad because he can't speak very well.

Me: Why does him not speaking well make you sad?

K: Because sometimes, when he wants to speak to people, he can't say what he wants to say very well.

Me: Do you think that bothers Jordan too?

K: Yes, because sometimes when he wants us to repeat what we said, we don't understand him, and it bothers him.

Me: Would you say it is challenging to have a brother with special needs?

K: What do you mean by that question?

Me: Does it make your life hard at home having a brother who needs so much attention?

Kaiyah: No.

Me: Do you ever feel like you aren't as important as Jordan?

K: Sometimes because you play with him more than you play with me.

Me: I want you to realize you are just as important as he is, okay? But you do understand why he gets a little more attention, right?

K: Yes, I do.

Me: Good. What are some things you like about having Jordan as a big brother?

K: Sometimes, I get to play with him. Sometimes we get to skate around the house with our skates, and we like it. It's fun.

Me: Does it make you feel special that Jordan wants to play with you sometimes even though he has a disability?

K: Yes, it does because I have no one that will play with me.

Me: Are there some things you don't like about having Jordan as a brother?

K: Sometimes, when we ask him to do something, it takes him a little while to do it. Like when we ask him to get out of the kitchen.

Me: And what about you specifically? Does he do things to you that you don't like that you know are because of his disability?

K: He pushes me sometimes, and I do not like that.

Me: Do you wish Jordan was like everyone else in the family?

K: Yes, because he could understand us better. And when we ask him to do something, he could probably do it better.

Me: Last question. Is there anything you want others to know about how you feel about Jordan and your relationship with him?

Kaiyah: I love him.

Me: And Jordan loves you too. I love you and glad that he has a little sister like you that looks after him.

K: Aww, thanks.

Chapter 23

"Guammah"

When my first grandson, Jordan, was born, I was excited for my daughter to have the son she always wanted.

When she went back to work, I had to be his babysitter for a brief time, but I remember that time vividly. It was when I noticed that he wouldn't make eye contact with me. I remember saying to my daughter, "He doesn't want to look at me." Every time I would look at him, he would turn away. When I would move to make eye contact with him, he'd turn the other way again. In my mind, I wondered why because he didn't do that to anyone else. I really felt as if he didn't like me, and he was only a few months old.

As time went on, he got used to me, but I still got no interaction from him as a grandchild would have with a grandmother. He wouldn't come close to me, so there were no hugs or kisses. I couldn't even get him to smile.

My daughter started to show concern for his development because he wasn't talking much and wouldn't eat different foods. He also started jumping around and making loud noises. Eventually, she shared with me she was concerned he may have autism and would have him evaluated.

He was diagnosed right before the age of 4. I now understood how he responded or didn't respond to me was nothing that I did. It was the disability that kept him disconnected from me. But now that we had learned there was a reason behind his different behaviors, things shifted.

I felt for my daughter. He was still my grandson no matter what, but she was his mother. She had to live this every day. I couldn't imagine what she was going through finding out she had a son who could never speak, learn how to use the bathroom, or do anything on his own a lot of us take for granted. It was because of those things I saw just how much love she had for him.

Time went on, and when he got to be around the age of 5 or 6, I noticed just how smart he was despite the diagnosis. He understood and did whatever you asked of him but couldn't respond verbally. He would point to the foods he wanted, but you knew what and when he wanted it for the most part.

He was such a sweet little boy. I couldn't understand how something so drastic could happen to him and our family. Not to say that there was something wrong with him, but it just wasn't normal. And I think that's what made him special.

I have watched my grandson grow from a quiet baby into an intelligent, fun, but a sneaky teenager. Jordan is 14 years old at the time of this book and has a personality like everyone else. Sometimes he acts his age, but he often does things a much younger child would do. Jordan is a happy boy but can get angry and will let you know it. He loves electronics and food, like most kids his age, and is very comical. He's our little comedian of few words.

The relationship I have with Jordan at this time is entirely different than it was in the past. Although it doesn't happen much anymore, he used to come into my room and lie with me, sometimes until he fell asleep. He speaks to me now, some occasions before I can talk to him, but not that often. He does allow me to hug him, and he will hug me back. Just recently, he kissed me on the cheek, which is not typical of him either.

We've come a long way from him turning the other way when I looked at him. I love who he is. He may have autism, but autism doesn't have him.

"iN cLOSinG"

Getting the perspective of the prominent people in Jordan's life has enlightened me. I pretty much know how his grandmother and little sister felt. But reading Sierra's story, I was taken aback.

I'd be lying if I said I didn't feel some way after reading what she sent me. I do understand that children don't view things as adults would and therefore can mistake the way I interact with Jordan as favoritism, but I must correct where she said I gave him both Wii systems when in fact, my mother gave me hers, so he wouldn't play with the one that they used. Unfortunately, when you have typical and atypical children, you will have this kind of misconstrue.

I am disappointed in myself that this happened, and I didn't do a better job balancing time, attention, and love between all my children so that she wouldn't have felt that way, so they wouldn't have thought he was the favorite. I have been trying to do better in recent days.

Since Jordan has been on the GAPS diet, I can't just go and pick up something quick for him. Therefore, I must make sure that he has soups, casseroles, eggs, vegetables, and herbs on hand always. Cooking for him so much caused me to neglect to prepare food for everyone else. When you make three kinds of soups and two different casseroles, fried onions, and scrambled eggs every morning, cooking dinner is the furthest thing from your mind because, to you, you have done so eight times in a week. Throw in making homemade sauerkraut and yogurt; I was tired of being in the kitchen.

I have since come up with something that takes care of everyone, even if it puts more of a strain on me every day. I think things would probably be a lot different if I only had to attend to my family. But I have a whole other family outside of this one—my church family.

The kids I help teach every Sunday, those who are a part of our Tuesday night Bible study, and our VIPs that come to give their parents respite every 4th Saturday of the month. Throw in assisting the facilitator in a discipleship class every Monday, meetings every 3rd Monday and 3rd Saturday, and meetings every two weeks to prepare for a prom for children with disabilities. I get tired just thinking about everything.

And the crazy thing about it is, this isn't the life I chose. No, no, no, this life picked me. Having a child with special needs isn't what I wanted for my life, but God wanted this for me to put me where I am today. I struggle and get tons of bumps and bruises daily. I get knocked down, but God picks me right back up. And when I think I don't have any more to give, He supplies me with the will to keep going. His word is true when it says God won't give you any more than you can bear.

"LaSt thOUghTs"

In my closing, I ended with how God won't give you more than you can bear. I didn't include a scripture reference because when looking it up, I kept being led to one that was slightly different in context. 1 Corinthians 10:13 (NIV) says, *"No temptation has overtaken you except what is common to mankind. And God is faithful; He will not let you be tempted beyond what you can bear. But when you are tempted, He will also provide a way out so that you can endure it."*

If you notice, the verse talks about being tempted, not about the adversity that falls on our lap. So, what do we do about that?

Well, I believe that whether an ungodly feeling or some other thing that tempted you is hard to handle, one thing remains. We must cast those burdens on God. *1 Peter 5:7, "Give all your worries and cares to God, for he cares about you."*

We tend to want to handle everything ourselves, which typically puts us in a worse position than when we started. But when we give it all to Him, He sees us through as *Psalm 55:22 (NIV)* states, *"Cast your cares on the Lord and He will sustain you; He will never let the righteous be shaken."*

In the past, I always felt like I needed to do things to control Jordan's behaviors. I kept him out of school, tried to discipline him, and never handed it over to God. I wanted a happy marriage but never sincerely asked Him to be at the center of it. Multiple things were going on in my life that were not good, but once I gave everything over to Him, peace came over me. I was no longer consumed with Jordan's negative behaviors of problems within my marriage. Letting Him take over allowed me to learn the tools I needed to face my issues. God just needs to be at the center of it all and not only included.

These are my last thoughts, and as I close this chapter of the book and about my fasting, I pray my testimonies will help you gain the knowledge you may need to face whatever may come your way. Whether you are a parent or a couple that has a child with special needs. A single mother or just someone is looking to gain guidance through Christ. Hopefully, the words in this book can lead you in the right direction on how to make God the center of your life. To live in the way God desires for you to live by seeking Him daily, denying yourself, praying, fellowshipping with others, and witnessing when you have a testimony. Oh, I can't forget, fasting.

www.ingramcontent.com/pod-product-compliance
Lightning Source LLC
Chambersburg PA
CBHW071157090426
42736CB00012B/2360